Light of the Upanishads

Light of the Upanishads

Abhaya Mudra Dasi

Light of the Upanishads

Cover paining by Abhaya Mudra Dasi

Copyright © 2024 Abhaya Mudra Dasi

abhaya_mudra2003@yahoo.com

All rights reserved.

ISBN: 978-0-9717717-3-4

DEDICATION

I dedicate this book to Shrila Prabhupada, who has so mercifully presented Shri Ishopanishad for the welfare of humanity. I beg for his mercy, and hope that this work will be pleasing to him.

His Divine Grace A.C. Bhaktivedanta Swami Prabhupada

Founder-Acharya of The International Society for Krishna Consciousness

TABLE OF CONTENTS

	Introduction: Up Close and Personal	Pg 1
1	**Chapter One:** The Reflected Reality	Pg 7
2	**Chapter Two:** The Yoga of the Upanishads	Pg 13
3	**Chapter Three:** Liberation from Bondage	Pg 18
4	**Chapter Four:** Mantra Yoga	Pg 24
5	**Chapter Five:** The "I" Factor	Pg 28
6	**Chapter Six:** The Avadhuta	Pg 37
7	**Chapter Seven:** Salvation from Delusion	Pg 48
8	**Chapter Eight:** The Gayatri Mantra	Pg 52
9	**Chapter Nine:** The Four Varnas and Ashramas	Pg 55
10	**Chapter Ten:** The Deepest Secret of All	Pg 60
	Afterword	Pg 62

Shri Shri Radha-Dharmeshwara

Abhaya Ashram

Introduction

Up Close and Personal

There is a modern saying that goes, "Up close and personal." In a word, this is the message of the *Upanishads*. "*Upanishad*" means "up close," because these teachings were imparted down through the ages from the *guru* to the disciple, while sitting face to face. And the ultimate Upanishadic message is personal. The *Upanishads* teach personalism, or the understanding that the Supreme Lord is a person, just as you and I are persons. The difference is that He is the Supreme Person, and we spirit souls are His individual parts and parcels. He is like the Sun, and we living entities are like the rays that emanate from the Sun. Therefore, as spiritual personalities we owe our eternal existence to Him. Our eternal position is meant to be one of subservience to the Supreme Person in a spirit of humble acquiescence. After all, the *Upanishads* were scribed by Sage Vyasadeva, the literary incarnation of God, Krishna, who is an *acharya* in our Vaishnava disciplic line. Therefore, there can be no question that the ultimate message of the *Upanishads* is one of finding God through personalism.

Nevertheless, to many readers of this ancient Vedic lore, the *Upanishads* appear to emphasize the impersonal feature of the Supreme Absolute Truth. Too often, a sense of "oneness beyond duality" becomes the student's conclusion, when he has not read with sufficient guidance into the soul of these divine texts. Yet, can God be merely a vast ocean of resplendent luminosity—or is He something more than an endlessly blazing luster that shines above this world of birth and death? Can the search for truth find its conclusion with a dispassionate merging into the brilliance of a divine shower of light? Is becoming "one" with the blinding effulgence of God the final goal of self-ralization? What lies beyond the white light that the impersonalists claim is their final destination? The *Upanishads* give the student both sides of the conundrum, yet the conclusion is one of personalism.

While the impersonalist seeks *sayuja mukti* to bathe in God's Brahmajyoti (the transcendental rays of the Supreme Lord Vishnu), the pure devotee revels in the bliss of devotional service at the feet of Shri Radha and Krishna in the transcendental world of Vrindavana. Although the road through the *Upanshads* is strewn here and there with trails in either direction—personalism versus impersonalism—in these pages, Shrimati Abhaya Mudra Dasi has illuminated the devotee's path to the actual goal of Vedic wisdom. Here, in *The Light of the Upanishads,* the reader will see with clarity that the ultimate Upanishadic message is one of pure devotional service to the Supreme Personality of Godhead in His most intimate form as Krishna.

Our Gaudiya Vaishnava *sampradaya* embraces this personalist school of thought. This disciplic line has descended from Shri Chaitanya Mahaprabhu, Who is none other than the Supreme Lord Krishna Himself in the mood of His own pure devotee. In the *Bhagavad-gita As It Is* (15.15), Krishna explains to Arjuna, "Of all the *Vedias* I am to be known." Since the *Upanishads* are derived from Vedic literature, this point alone establishes their message is one of personalism. The goal of the *Upanishads* is Krishna.

These teachings of the Gaudiya *acharyas* have been distributed all over the world by our Guru Maharaja, His Divine Grace A.C. Bhaktivedanta Swami Prabhupada. He personally planted the seeds of Krishna consciousness in over a hundred countries and through sixty volumes of literature, with translations going into over fifty languages. Through his divine dispensation of Krishna consciousness, Shrila Prabhupada has summarized and condensed the search for truth through the extraordinary mercy of Mahaprabhu's *sankirtana* movement.

Lord Shri Chaitanya taught that the ultimate conclusion of *achintya-bheda-abeda tattwa*, means that the Supreme Lord is both *bheda* and *abeda*, or "simultaneously, inconceivable one and different." Although, today the world is awash in a misconception of impersonal so-called "oneness with the Divine," this does not mean that the devotee fears investigating and understanding the monistic philosophy in a practical way. For the devotee, the endeavor to realize both aspects of the Absolute Truth side by side is essential in understanding Krishna consciousness.

There is an ocean of difference between the understanding of the Vaishnava servant of Krishna, and the so-called realization of the impersonalist, or Mayavadi, who thinks he has become "one with God." The devotee recognizes that the impersonal feature of Godhead is subservient to the personal understanding because the rays of the Brahmajyoti emanate from the transcendental body of Lord Vishnu. The view of the impersonalist, or monist, is actually abhorrent to the pure devotee, who considers that their path of "ego death" is a form of spiritual suicide.

The Mayavadi has turned this search for truth around and has understood everything backward. He rashly claims that Krishna has emanated from an ocean of divine light. This is not only impossible, but it defies common sense, because that which is void of senses cannot create that which is sensient. The ultimate truth is that Lord Krishna is the Supreme Personality of Godhead, while the rays of His body form the divine light that is sought by *yogis* and philosophers. Through many lifetimes they attempt to merge into an imaginary "oneness with God," yet even for those who become successful, their efforts are temporary. Impersonalists are like birds of prey who fly high into the sky, only to return to feast on the carrion of dead beasts. In the same way, the soul submerged in Mayavada lacks personal support, so he returns to this world of temporary personalities to perform activities of a mundane humanitarian nature or try to find pleasure in the senses again. On the other hand, devotees realize that, since we are infinitesimal parts and parcels of God, seeking Lord Krishna's shelter is the eternal, constitutional position of the living entity.

To convey the pure devotee's conclusion, or Vaishnava *siddhanta*, Shrila Prabhupada has given us his translation and commentary on the *Shri Ishopanishad*. *Shri Ishopanishad* condenses the essence of all Upanishadic teachings, as shown in verse 16:

> *pushann ekarshe yama surya prajapatya*
> *vyuha rashmin samuha tejo*
> *yat te rupam kalyana-tamam*
> *tat te pashyami yo 'sav asau purushah so 'ham asmi*

"O my Lord, O primeval philosopher, maintainer of the universe, O regulating principle, destination of the pure devotees, well-wisher of the progenitors of mankind, please remove the effulgence of Your transcendental rays so that I can see Your form of bliss. You are the eternal Supreme Personality of Godhead, like unto the sun, as am I."

Shrila Prabhupada illuminates this verse, and gives the essence of Upansiadic wisdom, in his Bhaktivedanta Purport: "The *brahmajyoti* is described in the *Brahma Samhita* as the rays emanating from that supreme spiritual planet, Goloka Vrindavana, just as the Sun's rays emanate from the Sun globe. Until one surpasses the glare of the *brahmajyoti,* one cannot receive information of the land of the Lord. The impersonalist philosophers, blinded as they are by the dazzling *brahmajyoti,* can realize neither the factual abode of the Lord, nor His transcendental form. Limited by their poor fund of knowledge, such impersonalist thinkers cannot understand the all-blissful transcendental form of Lord Krishna. In this prayer, therefore, *Shri Ishopanishad* petitions the Lord to remove the effulgent rays of the *brahmajyoti* so that the pure devotee can see His all-blissful transcendental form."

Shri Krishna in His Abode of Goloka Vrindavana

Here in *Light of the Upanishads*, Shrimati Abhaya Mudra Dasi pursues this radiant path, upon which our previous *acharyas* have so brilliantly shined their light of wisdom. Becoming one with God does not mean to become God, as many impersonalists believe. Rather, it means to retain the eternal uniqueness of one's personal soul, while becoming "one with the will of God." Following the path of the *Upanishads*, therefore, means to know that finding God, or coming to Krishna consciousness, entails not only understanding His brilliant rays, but going beyond His effulgence to the shelter of His lotus feet. The Supreme Person is Krishna, and we are His eternal servants. As Prabhupada would say, "Krishna means two—

Krishna and you!"

-Patita Pavana dasa Adhikary

I

The Reflected Reality

In *Shri Chaitanya Charitamrita* (*Adi Lila* 4.50-51), the author Shrila Krishnadasa Kaviraja writes, "Therefore Lord Gauranga, who is Shri Hari Himself, accepted the sentiments of Radha, and thus fulfilled His own desires. Lord Chaitanya is the shelter of the demigods, the goal of the *Upanishads*, the be-all and end-all of the great sages, the beautiful shelter of His devotees, and the essence of the love of the lotus-eyed *gopis*. Will He again be the object of my vision?"

Shri Chaitanya Mahaprabhu

In the *Maitreya Upanishad*, Lord Shiva states that the liberated soul is also known as "*chaitanya*." Each individual soul is part and parcel of Lord Vishnu, or Shri Krishna, the Supreme Personality of Godhead, and through this basic realization, the aspirant can reach the initial stages of the impersonal aspect of the Supreme Absolute

Truth.

However, real oneness with everything that exists is found only in the personality of the omnipresent Supreme Lord since He is the proprietor of everything, and everything resides in Him. Thus, to give a hint of His position, Lord Chaitanya Mahaprabhu accepted the fourth order of life, or *sannyasa*, the highest level of renunciation, from the impersonal school, and there He received the name "Chaitanya." One meaning of Chaitanya is "awareness of the Self."

Only the Supreme Lord can be completely aware of His Own Self. Therefore, we individual *jiva* souls should accept the aspect of oneness with the Self—or Krishna in the heart in the form of Paramatma—in the same way that a true wife considers her husband as her very self. Through sharing love, two individuals can feel a sense of being "one soul in two bodies," just as Lord Shiva appears along with Parvati as half male and half female in the form of Ardhanarishvara.

Shri Ardhanishwara

Although the impersonalists look to the *Upanishads* to try to merge into the Supreme Absolute, the true essence of Upanishadic oneness is found in the oneness of shared love. Revealed *shastra* teaches its lessons gradually, and often through hints. As an example, in the *Bible* (Matthew 7:6-7) it is written:

> "Do not give what is holy to dogs, nor cast thy pearls before swine, lest they trample them under their feet, and turn and tear you into pieces. Ask, and it shall be given to you. Seek, and you shall find it. Knock, and it will be opened to you."

The *Upanishads* forbid imparting wisdom unto those who are not worthy. Even so, the great Vaishnava *acharyas*, who are true teachers and upholders of the Absolute Truth, will often risk preaching God's message to the unworthy. By dint of a devotee's causeless mercy, sometimes a the low-born person can become a worthy recipient of the Absolute Truth.

However, as we have seen from the example of Shrila Prabhupada, the spiritual master of the worldwide Hare Krishna Movement, a *guru* may endure much suffering due to unauthorized activities of immature disciples. Indeed, many such neophytes misused the *guru's* freely-shared knowledge of Krishna consciousness for their own illicit purposes. Instead of pursuing the path of liberation from *samsara* to escape the miseries of material existence, posers in the dress of devotees exploited the *guru-vani* they received, in order to gain worldly power and riches. Such disciples who misuse the mercy of the bona fide spiritual master risk dragging their *guru* down along with them.

Our consciousness, or *chitta,* is the cause of remembrance, and for our meditation on the past. This is the sole reason why the *jiva* must undergo *samsara,* repeated birth and death here in this material world. According to the *Maitreya Upanishad*, instead of meditating on ever-changing and temporary things, a true seeker should meditate on Paramatma—or the immovable Self of all selves. The immortal self does not go anywhere, even when the body is transferred through space. In its pure form, the immortal self is even more fixed than Dhruvaloka, the abode of Lord Vishnu within this material universe around which the whole universe, with its *kakachakra*, or zodiac of planets and stars, revolves.

Yet, in due course of time, even the location of Dhruvaloka also changes. This is the reason why Lord Vishnu sought the most qualified devotee to accept the position of leadership upon the immovable star. Dhruva means "fixed," and the Lord recognized that Dhruva Maharaja was the most worthy, due to his fixed attention upon the Absolute Truth.

As described in *Bhagavad-gita As It Is* (15.1-2), this world is a reflection of the spiritual world:

> "The Blessed Lord said: There is a banyan tree which has its roots upward, and its branches down, and whose leaves are the Vedic hymns. One who knows this tree is the knower of the *Vedas*.
>
> "The branches of this tree extend downward and upward, nourished by the three modes of material nature. The twigs are the objects of the senses. This tree also has roots going down, and these are bound to the fruitive actions of human society."

Thus, whatever we see in this world should be understood to be a reflection. The reflection, or the reflector, is the female principle of the Absolute; while the reflected is the male principle. Although a devotee can find God even here in this material world, one must be a keen observer, for the physical body itself carries the principles of reflector and reflected.

Each one of us has two sides which, according to the *Upanishads*, are female and male in nature. Thus, every person has a male-right and female-left half of the body. Everyone has a left and a right hand, a left and a right leg, a left and a right nostril, and so on. Every person is meant to have a balance of male and female qualities in himself or herself.

However, some organs are single in nature, like the gender-specific reproductive organs, or the mouth, which are means for interaction with others. A male will want to have a female to interact with for physical sexual union, while the mouth will exchange sounds with others, and take in food from the surrounding world. Such interactions are reflections of the original principle of love, which is meant for exchanges between the self, which is female in nature, and the Self, which is male in nature.

In this way, food is not meant for selfish enjoyment. Rather, it is meant for exchanging love, for only through offering everything to God will pure love manifest. The *Upanishads* state that anyone who does not offer his food to the Supreme Self (Krishna), eats only sin. Krishna says the same in *Bhagavad-gita* (9.27), where He advises Arjuna that everything the devotee does and eats should be offered to Him exclusively.

> "O son of Kunti, all that you do, all that you eat, all that you offer and give away, as well as all austerities that you may perform, should be done as an offering unto Me."

The fourth *valli* of *Katha Upanishad* (verse 10) states, "Whatever is here, that is there. Whatever is there, that again is here. The person obtains death who seems to see a difference here." The soul does not move in space when the body moves. Everything is already here and the person, the soul, who experiences death also does not venture anywhere, although in his mind he thinks he is roving. *Katha Upanishad* (verses 11-12) continues, "By the mind, indeed, is this realization attained that there is no difference at all! The confused one goes from death to death and seems to see a difference here. However, a Person, who measures the size of a thumb, Paramatma, stands in the mind of one's self. One is always connected to Him. This, verily, is That!"

II

Yoga of the Upanishads

Our need is to connect to this eternal Supreme Person, who sits in the heart of each embodied soul. He is brilliant and unaffected by the smoke of material contamination. He is the guide of all living entities, and He is their inspiration to act in certain ways, according to their *karma*, and also to free them from *karma* once they are ready.

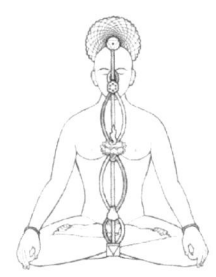

There are a hundred and one channels that emanate from the heart, where the Supersoul stands within each of us. One of these channels leads up to the crown of the head. A person whose consciousness can climb up that channel can become liberated at the time of death. Since life comes through *prana,* or the life breath, it also goes out back to Prana—personified as the Supreme Lord Who is the source of *prana*. The person who knows this is already liberated.

In the body, there are five vital airs: (1) *prana*, or the incoming breath, (2) *apana*, or the outgoing breath, (3) *samana*, or the air in the stomach, (4) *vyana*, or the air that circulates throughout the body, and (5) *udana*, or the air that goes upwards.

Prana is born from the *atman*, the pure soul, and establishes itself in the eyes, ears, and mouth. *Apana* is situated in the excretion and the organs for procreation. *Samana* is the middle equalizing air, or rather the lack of air. Food is offered to this breath and the seven *chakras* are powered by it. From the main hundred and one channels in the heart, seventy-two secondary channels spread throughout the body as the seat of *vyana* or the circulatory air. *Udana* is the air created by good work. It makes one light and it pushes the soul upwards to liberation.

 The *Prana Upanishad* describes the meaning of AUM or OM: Whoever meditates on A comes to the earthly plane after death. Whoever meditates on the A+U goes to the world of the *pitris*. And, whoever does not differentiate between the different elements of AUM, and meditates on all sounds equally, goes to the world of Brahman. The sound OM is the union of male and female energies. When one speaks, there is no breath, and thus the primeval sound OM vibrates beyond the scope of material breath. Whoever focuses on OM, or its extended and personal version, the Hare Krishna *mahamantra*, at the time of death, becomes liberated.

Shri Krishna states in *Bhagavad-gita As It Is* (10.25) *giram asmy ekam aksaram giram*, which translates as, "Of vibrations I am the transcendental OM."

In the *Mandukya Upanishad*, OM is associated with the three states of existence: A is for the walking state. This walking state is actually the past, since everything that we see has already happened, and we are merely reflecting on it. The sleep  state is associated with U, or the state representing the actual present situation in its wholeness. Here, one can get lost in the dream state because everything happens simultaneously. The sound of M is associated with deep sleep, or the future, since we always imagine a blissful future without any problems.

In *Mandukya Upanishad* (7), it is stated that the soul should be differentiated from all these states because he is beyond all these three states. The nature of the *atma,* or the soul, is to be united with the Self, to be unchanging or without a desire to develop something in itself or around itself, tranquil, gentle, and unique. There are three births for the soul. When one is conceived, when one is born from the mother, and when one dies. Death can be the real birth for the one who has realized his true identity as a servant of the Supreme Lord Shri Krishna, since death can give birth to a transcendental reality for the self-realized.

The *Brihadaranyaka Upanishad* states that there are two forms of Brahman. One is formless, while the other one is with form. The formless Brahman is exhibited by the all-pervasive wind, while the form of Brahman with the form is seen in the Sun. Sunlight is actually the representation of the spiritual effulgence that is seen in the material world emanating from the body of the Supreme Lord. Thus, the Sun is also known as Surya-Narayan. The light of the Sun vibrates the sound OM. Whoever mediates on the Sun at sunrise, mid-day, and at the time of Sunset, while uttering the primeval Gayatri *mantra* with understanding, becomes liberated from birth and death.

Poetry once consisted of the strict meters of *mantras* that produced tangible results. Later the rhythm of the *mantras* became classified into different rhythms and meaningful sounds, and thus songs and praise were written according to strict rules. However, in Kali Yuga, rhyming became a fob for poetical expression, which has nothing to do with the actual purpose of poetry. In Vedic poetry, every word has a meaning, and each one can manifest a tangible result. Yet, now we have come to a time when poetry does not even rhyme any longer, and it is used merely to express the mental debris that has become accumulated due to the pressures caused by material nature.

OM in and of itself is pure poetry. OM is the source of the universe, and is integrated within universe itself. Devotees who meditate on OM, or who always chant *Hare Krishna Hare Krishna Krishna Krishna Hare Hare, Hare Rama Hare Rama Rama Rama Hare*

Hare, will return back to the source of bliss.

In the section entitled *The Light of Man is the Soul* (verse 22), the *Brihadaranyaka Upanishad* describes the blissful state which is difficult to explain, "This, verily, is that form of his, which is beyond desires, is free from evil, and is without fear. As a man, when in the embrace of his beloved wife, knows nothing within or without, so this person, when in the embrace of the intelligent Supersoul, knows nothing within or without. Verily, this is his true form in which his desire is satisfied, in which the Supersoul is his desire, in which he is without desire and without sorrow."

Generally, the subject of love is not much prevalent in the *Upanishads,* which deal mostly with approaching the spiritual reality. Yet, here is a description of the love that the soul and the Supersoul share with each other. Indeed, many so-called "renunciates" have not understood the meaning of renunciation. True renunciation is the path of purification in order to find this love. In this search, a true renunciate must forego everything, including his possessions and family, as well as his desires for fame, money, and sense gratification. He may be seen to behave like a madman or a beggar, although he is neither. A *yogi* who accepts the position of a renunciate, yet who does not follow these rules of renunciation, becomes truly lost.

Sometimes the sign of true realization is that a renunciate does not speak. Since the spiritual reality that he has seen and experienced is impossible to explain to laymen, who are engaged in temporary activities, he remains silent. Still, in front of worthy listeners, he will exhibit eloquence and poetic ability in guiding others to the Supreme Absolute Truth.

In the *Svetasvatara Upanishad* (9-10) there are additional details about the relationship between the soul and the Supreme Lord, "There are two unborn ones: the knowing Lord and the unknowing individual soul, the omnipotent and the impotent. *Prakriti* is also unborn, and is connected both with the enjoyer and the object of enjoyment. The soul is infinite, universal, and inactive. When one finds out about this triad, he understands Brahman. What is perishable, is the primary matter, or *pradhana*. What is immortal and imperishable is Hara, the seat of the soul. God rules over both the perishable and the imperishable. By meditating upon Him, by uniting with Him more and more, finally, there is cessation from every illusion."

Focusing upon the Supreme is achieved through the mind, according to the *Bhramabindu Upanishad.* There, Lord Brahma explains that the mind can be either pure or impure. When one is free from material passions and desires, then one can become liberated, even in this very existence. The eternal, spiritual reality is automatically revealed to the purified.

Lord Brahma

A conditioned soul carries a sense of "I am" because of *ahankara* or ego. *Chitta,* or consciousness, gives him memory, intelligence, and the concept of different forms. Ultimately, the mind is the seat of desires. Because the objects of desire form in the mind, when one no longer creates material objects in his mind, he can qualify for liberation.

III

Liberation from Bondage

In these troubled times of Kali Yuga, sinister powers take advantage of the mental weaknesses of the masses. Through the internet, movies, advertisements, books, and other means, demonic individuals create images of desire to exploit people for their profits. Yet, those who learn to meditate on the super-excellent form of Shri Krishna, will no longer be attracted to the temporary objects of desire. Thus, devotees of the Lord are free from the powers of manipulation and greed.

Chanting the Hare Krishna *mahamantra* is the best means for liberating the mind. One should always chant:

*Hare Krishna Hare Krishna Krishna Krishna Hare Hare
Hare Rama Hare Rama Rama Rama Hare Hare*

The word "man" derives from the Sanskrit *mana* for "mind." This indicates that the human mind is very strong, because human intelligent can create objects of desire through imagination that are specifically meant for enjoyment. However, the *atma,* or soul, is neither a man nor a woman; it is neither a human, a demigod, nor an animal. Although the *atma* transcends material bondage, the mind is the cause of the entity's suppression in the prison house of matter. The unfortunate person who doubts that liberation is within his grasp will never achieve freedom from the material dilemma. A person must understand that the desires of the individual *atma* are the cause of either his bondage or liberation. However, the Lord Himself is the ultimate liberator, and it is His decision when liberation will take place. Therefore, one should not focus on liberation as a goal but rather fully surrender at the lotus feet of the Lord. Attracting the attention of the Supreme Lord through devotional service is the only way out of *samsara*.

In the *Subal Upanishad*, the Lord tells Raikva, who was the first to receive the knowledge of Brahman from Brahma, that the soul itself is the cause of its own bondage. The *atma,* or self, creates the world in which it lives. Before the creation, there was only *tamas*, and from *tamas* came *rajas* and *sattva*, and the different elements of speech, along with everything we see and experience. The *atma* itself splits into male and female. Thus, in this world, one feels empty until he meets the other part of the self, or the one who represents the Self, the Lord. The person who is to be liberated must undo whatever has been done. He must merge his *prana* into the Universal air, just as Shri Krishna states that in *Bhagavad-gita As It Is* (4.29) *prana praneshu juhvati*. Whatever one merges into, or mediates upon, he becomes that thing. If one mediates on Shri Krishna, he may qualify himself for going back to Krishna. The *yogi* who understands that he is part and parcel of the Lord, does not release his breath at the time of death. Rather, his breath remains within the self, merging into its own existence. Lord Brahma, the first living entity within the universe, states in the final verse of the *Subal Upanishad*, "This *Subala-bija, Brahma Upanishad* should neither be given outright, nor taught to one who has not controlled his passions. It should not be taught to one who has no sons, or who has not accepted a spiritual master or, having become his disciple, has not resided with him for a year. Additionally, it should not be taught to one whose family and conduct are not known. These doctrines should be taught only to that person who has supreme devotion unto the Lord, and to his *guru*. Only then can this truth shine within his heart. Such is the elucidation on the way to Nirvana. Such is the exposition of the *Vedas*, verily this is the right presentation of the *Vedas*." The *Upanishads* make it clear that without accepting a bona fide spiritual master, a *guru*, no one can advance in spiritual knowledge. Lord Shri Krishna repeats this advice in *Bhagavad-gita As It Is* (4.34):

"Just try to learn the truth by approaching a spiritual master. Inquire from him submissively, and render service unto him. The self-realized soul can impart knowledge unto you because he has seen the truth."

Shri Guru Parampara

Upanishad means "close to the *guru*." One should not think that merely reading the *Upanishads* can be a substitute for accepting a *guru*, who is learned in the Supreme Absolute Truth. The *Upanishads* mostly describe the impersonal aspect of the Absolute Truth, or the concept of Sat or Brahman. Only here and there do the *Upanishads* hint at the personal aspect of Godhead, which lies beyond the great curtain of spiritual light emanating from the Lord's all-transcendental body. The *yogi*, who merges himself into the all-pervasive Brahman, temporarily removes the fetters of material bondage. Yet, the journey does not end there. The seeker must "unmerge" himself, even as he enters into the other side, and into a transcendental existence. He must continue onward in awareness of his eternal personal identity. Shri Krishna's supreme position as the Source of the all-pervasive spiritual reality is unimaginable by material standards. The actual experience of the Supreme Personality of Godhead Krishna can only be revealed by a *guru* who has seen the Truth with his own eyes. The transcendental books like the *Upanishads* cannot replace the personal association with the *guru*. Rather, they serve as an introduction to the *guru*. They are never an independent guide on the path of transcendence, although they are written by the *guru*.

Qualifications are required to understand who is a *guru*, just as the *guru* himself must be qualified to impart knowledge to the sincere seeker. In the Vedic times, there was a well-established culture of knowing beforehand the qualities of a potential *guru*, then testing and recognizing who is qualified to serve as a spiritual master. On the other hand, today the teacher is known by a designation, and people generally believe that knowledge can be purchased with money. Today, neither the student knows how to seek out a *guru*, nor does the real *guru* canvass for disciples. The *guru* will remain a secret, revealing himself only before the disciple who is qualified to find him.

For example, although His Divine Grace A.C. Bhaktivedanta Swami Prabhupada stands as a giant amongst *gurus*, still few persons outside of the Hare Krishna society have any idea who started this worldwide *sankirtana* movement. Some believe that the Hare Krishna movement is a sort of fashion or trend that spontaneously burst out of nowhere. Yet the founder-*acharya*, Shrila Prabhupada, originally gave the world the first *Upanishad,* known as *Shri Ishopanishad. Shri Ishopanishad* is the introduction to all of the other *Upanishads*. Just as the first canto of *Shrimad-Bhagavatam* serves the reader as the overview of the entire *Bhagavata Purana*, in the same way *Shri Ishopanishad* condenses many of the topics of the other *Upanishads*.

While the curious seeker may be tempted to dive further into the other *Upanishads*, they should be studied under the careful guidance of a bona fide spiritual master. Venturing alone into the world of the *Upanishads* can distort the mind, and one can find himself in unknown and dangerous territories.

Some of the *Upanishads* reveal different practices for attaining bliss, even while the soul is embodied. In the *Shuka Rahasya Upanishad*, Lord Shiva teaches Shukadeva Goswami the ancient practice of folding of the hands as a salutation to the Chatura-vyuha, or four forms of Lord Narayana. The touching of the thumbs is a salutation to Vasudeva; touching of the index fingers is a salutation to Sankarshana; touching of the middle fingers is a salutation to Pradyumna; touching of the ring fingers is a salutation to Aniruddha, and the touching of the little fingers again is a salutation to the totality expression of Godhead in the first representation of the Absolute, or Vasudeva. Thus, folding the hands in prayer represents the union of the Chatura-vyuha, which are the four expressions of the Absolute Truth, whether in the spiritual or in the material worlds.

The fingers also represent the five elements: the thumb represents earth; the index finger represents fire; the middle finger represents water; the ring finger represents air; and the little finger represents ether. Thus, the folding of the hands represents the union of the elements, and just by folding hands in prayer, one can realize the Absolute.

The *Tejo-Bindu Upanishad* states that the process of controlling the breath for the ignorant means closing only one's nostrils. However, those in knowledge know that breath control means meditating with undivided attention upon the Absolute Truth, which is entirely an internal process. This process is best attained by chanting the Hare Krishna *mahamantra*. The sound vibration that is produced when chanting the Names of the Lord automatically controls the breathing process. This *mantra* should be chanted always. There are many obstacles to constantly chanting the *mahamantra,* including laziness, attraction to other things, offenses, and so on. However, one can overcome them all simply by enthusiastically inquiring into the Absolute Truth.

The *atman,* or individual spirit soul, is beyond any worldly description. The *guru* stands at the border between the explicit and inexplicit. Thus, he is the only one who can describe the indescribable. According to *Dvaya Upanishad, gu* means darkness," and *ru* means "the guardian." Therefore, *guru* means, "he who guards against darkness."

Thus, the *guru* gives light and opens the eyes of the student to help him understand his real position. Without a proper *guru*, one cannot attain salvation. The *guru* is the *acharya*, because he sets the example of right action. He gives the student the means to know the difference between *sat* (eternal), and *asat* (temporary). He teaches us to realize what is relative, and what is eternal.

IV

Mantra Yoga

The Personality of Godhead Lord Vishnu

In *Jabaladarshan Upanishad*, Lord Vishnu describes the four ways of *yoga* that are the means of attaining the Supreme. These are *mantra yoga*; *laya yoga*; *hatha yoga* (which is known by its eight sections), and *raja yoga*. In this day and age, when people are short-lived and cannot concentrate for an extended period, the method of *mantra yoga* is the only practical means of controlling the mind in the practice of *yoga*. Despite *mantra yoga* being the most practical and easiest approach to *yoga* in this age, it must be practiced for at least twelve years in order to approach perfection. Although beginners on the spiritual path often become attracted to many different *mantras*, a sincere practitioner should concentrate on one, the *mantra* that Lord Chaitanya has given for this day and age. Simply by chanting the Hare Krishna *mahamantra*, the devotee can achieve all perfection in this life, and go back to Godhead at the end of it.

In *Trisikhi-Brahmanopanishad,* the Sun demigod further elaborates on some elements of the eightfold system of *hatha yoga*:

The first stage is *yama*, control, or the process through which the soul detaches from the body. This is achieved through non-violence, truthfulness, celibacy, kindness, simplicity, forgiveness, patience, dietary restrictions, purity, and freedom from greed.

The second stage of *hatha yoga* is *niyama*, which is the process of developing a loving and all-permeating attitude towards the Absolute. This love for God is developed through penance, inner satisfaction, developing godly qualities though religiosity, generosity, meditation on God, reading the *Vedas*, modesty, wit, chanting *mantras*, and resolution.

Lord Surya-Narayana, the Sun Demigod

The third stage of *hatha* yoga is *asana*, which is characterized by proper association with the elements, and by understanding that one is not the doer. This is achieved by practicing different postures, which leads to complete control over the body's nerves. The three processes described above are supposed to make the body and mind very light and flexible.

The Sun demigod continued, the fourth step is *pranayama*. *Pranayama* involves understanding the fallacious nature of this universe, and is achieved through various breathing techniques. *Pranayama* can be performed only after the previous three stages have been perfected.

Pratyahara is the process of removing the scenes from the sense objects through the means of *asana* and *pranayama*. The practitioner should pull the sense away from all eighteen sensitive areas in the body, namely (1) the large toes of the feet, (2) the ankles, (3) the middle part of the pubic area, (4) the middle part of the genital organs, (5) the reproductive organs, (6) the root portion of the anus, (7) the heart, (8) the naval, (9) the throat, (10) the elbows, (11) the root of the pallet, (12) the root portion of the nose, (13) the eyeballs, (14) the middle portion of the brows, (15) the forehead, (16) the root portion of the brain, (17) the root portion of the hands, and (18) the root portion of the knees. In this way, the mind is ready to focus solely on the spiritual reality within.

Next comes the process of *dharana* when the *yogi* concentrates on the Absolute sitting in the mind. *Dratyahara* is achieved through meditation on the different forms of the Lord, as They are positioned in the *chakras* of the body, and through understanding the elements associated with the *chakras*. In this stage, one transforms the body from material to spiritual, as he sees how every part of the body is associated with the spiritual essence of the Lord in different ways.

Having forcefully concentrated on the previous stage on the object of meditation, on the next stage of *dyana* one can meditate on the

Lord without strain. At this stage, the practitioner should observe how his soul exists beyond the influences of the three limited stages of existence, namely, the waking, dreaming, and dreamless states, and how he is part of the spiritual reality of the Supreme. The Lord's endless form shines in absolute knowledge beyond imagination and beyond reach. His form is infinite, pleasing, omnipresent, illustrious and stands in sovereign power.

The final stage is *samadhi* means that, instead of reflecting on past experiences, the mind becomes constantly engaged in meditation upon the Lord. The devotee who has completely abandoned worldly passions, and who is selflessly engaged in the loving service of the Lord, has achieved *samadhi* and is a *jivanmukta,* or liberated person, even in the present body. Upon leaving this world of *samsara*, such a liberated devotee never returns to the mortal world. The chanting of the Hare Krishna *mahamantra* is ultimately meant to lead the practitioner to the same result as achieved by the *hatha yogi*. It is a fact that constant concentration upon the *mahamantra* leads to *samadhi*. How, then, do we concentrate upon the Absolute Truth?

V

The "I" Factor

The *Sita Upanishad*, whose focus is the glorification of Queen Sitadevi, the wife of Lord Rama, states that She is the sense of "I". The *Upanishads* teach that Vishnu is the "I am" factor—the eternal *sat* principle and Self of existence. Sita devi is *Yogamaya*, or the goddess of transcendental illusion, from whom the individual sense of "I" is eternally separated from the Lord. In this way, Lord Vishnu and His consort have become two separate individuals, even though there is no beginning or end to this process. The female principle, as a separated individual from the Lord, interacts back with the Lord, and by Her reflection of Him. He understands His own individuality, which otherwise is all-encompassing and is thus singular.

In *Bhagavad-gita As It Is* (15.13), Shri Krishna states *somo bhutva rasa-atmakah*, which means that the Moon (being female in nature) creates individuality in all living beings. In the material universe, this quality of individuality applies to the bodies of the embodied entities. However, it is the female principle that creates the partition even in the Absolute. In other words, the goddess's energy is also responsible for the manifestation of the limitless, eternal individuality of all living entities. It is this manifestation of different individualities that forms the playground for love, which is the supreme reason for existence in the Absolute. Thus, meditation upon the Lord as the principles of supreme male and female energies, is not like thinking of the ordinary attractions that exist between mundane males and females. Even so, the mundane has its roots in the Absolute love experienced by Shri Radha and Krishna.

There are many different means for achieving life's ultimate goal of pure love of God, and in fact many of these are hidden in the *Upanishads* mystical *shlokas*. In the different *yugas*, or divisions of time in this material world, there are various prescribed means of self-realization. In the Satya Yuga, the means was meditation, while in Tretya Yuga the goal was achieved through sacrifices, or *yagna*. In Dwapara Yuga, spiritual advancement was achieved through temple worship, including the worship of different forms of the Supreme Lord, writing *yantras*, practicing *tantra* (esoteric rituals), and so on. In Kali Yuga, the chanting of the Holy Names of God is prescribed, while for this current Kali Yuga, specifically the chanting of Hare Krishna *mahamantra* is prescribed.

The meaning of Rama in the Hare Krishna *mahamantra* is multifold. *Ra* is the spiritual light that emanates from the divine body of the Lord, while *Ma* is the source of this light. Rama represents the light of the soul, and by chanting Rama, one can understand his true position. Krishna is the Supreme, all-attractive Lord, while Hare is His internal potency. In the Hare Krishna *mahamantra,* we see the extended and more intimate meaning of AUM, wherein A stands for Brahma, U for Vishnu, and M for Rudra. Brahma is the creation, Vishnu is the maintenance, and Rudra is the destruction.

As quoted by Shrila Prabhupada (CC Adi.7.128, Purport), Shrila Rupa Goswami, explains that A stands for Krishna, U for Radha, and M for the living entity:

a-kareṇocyate krishnah sarva-lokaika-nayakah
u-kareṇocyate ma-karo jiva-vacakah radha.

On the absolute spiritual plane, where there is no destruction, Hare stands for the internal potency of Lord Krishna, who is Radha. Rama not only stands for Lord Vishnu as the King of Ayodhya, but Rama also means Lord Balarama who is the first expansion of Lord Krishna. Further, Rama represents the soul in its pure existence.

According to the *Mandala Brahmana Upanishad*, there are five defects in the body: (1) passion, (2) outward breathing, (3) anger, (4) sleep, and (5) fear. Each of these five stains can be controlled: passion through abnegation of desires; outward breathing through moderate food intake; anger through forgiveness; sleep through understanding the different *tattvas* (or elements) of creation and the Absolute; and fear through careful observation. Following these five will make one's existence pleasant, even here in this world of ignorance and constant danger.

Sandilya Upanishad further elaborates upon the eight-fold *yoga* system, and focuses on the results exhibited through the practice. The *Bhakti Rasamrita Sindhu* of Shrila Rupa Goswami follows a similar path, yet from the point of view of *bhakti yoga*. The great *acharya* first describes the rules and regulations that one must follow both in daily life, and in temple worship. He then focuses upon the development of knowledge, and on the means of focusing the mind. Although he explains *samadhi,* he even goes beyond that with his explanation of the five *rasas* (tastes), or relationships between the living entity and the Supreme Lord.

The *Paingada Upanishad* explains that liberation is obtained when the individual sees that everything belongs to Shri Krishna, and that the person (the individual soul) owns nothing. On the other hand, the concept of ownership—of "mine and yours"—leads to bondage. Only the seeker who has cleared away the bondage of *karma* that has piled up after unlimited births can reach the state of *samadhi*. In this state of "fixed mind," the enlightened *yogi* becomes undisturbed by any mundane thoughts and realizes his original personality.

One symptom of the mind that has become liberated from material entanglement is sleeping without dreaming. In the dream state, the *atma* withdraws the senses even as he simultaneously remembers incidents from his waking state, although these are recollected in a random fashion. The active state is when one creates *karma* through his attachment to this temporary world. Once the seeker has left behind the dream state, he can go deeper into *sushupti,* or deep sleep. He may even continue onward to a state that is similar to death when all organs, including mundane thoughts and intelligence, are completely withdrawn.

Only through complete purification of the mind, intelligence, and false ego can one see the Supreme Lord, Shri Krishna face to face. Such a state, the highest form of *yoga*, is beyond the mundane concept of knowledge and experience. In order to regain knowledge of the eternal Self, the seeker must completely abandon the deluding concept of the mundane self that is mired in the three modes of nature. This process of advancement through *yoga* could seem frightening to the mundane individual. However, it is very much like the process of falling in love, wherein one loses himself only to gain the wonderful feeling of surrender to the person he loves. The seeker must be encouraged to overcome his trepidations in his search for liberation, while ignoring self-realization only leads to perpetual *samsara* here in the world of birth and death.

As explained in the *Mana Upanishad*, the mind is the sole culprit for the living entity's bondage. Under the direction of Lord Vishnu, this world is created out of the imagination of the firstborn Brahma. Similarly, anyone who is created by Brahma, and who carries to some the qualities of his creator is, in some capacity, engaged in the process of creation. Therefore, by believing in the validity of the created objects, the person continues forming attachments to them. In this way, one becomes trapped within the creation of his mind.

Shri Radha and Krishna

A modern example can be given. Most people believe that money can buy anything, therefore, practically everyone is attached to procuring wealth. However, hypothetically, there could have been another belief system that would have entangled the masses with equal validity. Mundane knowledge exists only to justify how the living entity has become entrapped by a belief system that reflects blind faith in the money system, or any other material concept. The mind is especially powerful, as it is an expression of the thoughts that are rooted in mass consciousness. The mind is an expression of Aniruddha, because the mind is the representation of the supreme mind of the Lord. Once the devotee focuses his mind on serving Lord Shri Krishna, and avoids placing his faith in this temporary *jagat,* or universe, he moves towards liberation. To obtain emancipation, the devotee must focus on understanding that, "I am not this body; I am pure spirit soul, a minute part and parcel of the Supreme Lord Krishna."

Pure is the mind that, without any attachment for the results, dedicates all thoughts and activities with great sensitivity for the pleasure of the Lord. The pure mind provides and maintains the self, but does not contrive any resolutions that only cause further attachment. As explained by the Supreme Lord Shri Krishna (Bg 5.10). one must become *padma-patram ivambhasa*. He tells Arjuna, "One who performs his duty without attachment, surrendering the results unto the Supreme God, is not affected by sinful action, as the lotus leaf is untouched by water."

Even when the devotee is constantly active in this world, he does not become touched by the allegorical mud of material attachments because he has surrendered to Krishna. Unnecessary bonds become destroyed by avoiding speculations on the nature of the Supreme Absolute Truth. By transcending attachments, the absolute nature of the spirit soul begins to naturally emanate. Thus, by being constantly engaged in the service of Shri Krishna, the devotee steadily rises to the state of liberation. In the initial stages, one can engage in the worship of the Deity of the Lord. This process is called *saguna*, or seeing the Lord in the Deity only. However, when one advances, he can become *nirguna,* and transcend the state of merely being attached to the localized form of the Lord. The advanced practitioner sees the personal presence of the Lord everywhere, and engages accordingly

One should take the course of action that comes easily to him while avoiding over-endeavor, since over-endeavor always becomes the cause for new resolutions. Thus, attachments, which have bound the butterfly-like soul in a cocoon of endless threads from time immemorial, become vanquished through devotional service.

The mind that is attached to material nature can be elevated through the mind itself, just as one thorn is removed with the help of another thorn. It is easy to abandon temptations through understanding that we do not own anything. Only a pure and dispassionate temptation for devotional service should remain, since such an attraction comes solely from Paramatma, and can result in emancipation.

The attitude of "I am small, I am minute," will also help the seeker on the path of liberation. Through his internal balance, the devotee frees himself from mundane passions, even as he outwardly continues to comply with all worldly traditions and etiquette. He abandons anger, although externally he may exhibit it for the sake of correcting others. He abandons his false ego as well, although outwardly may still exhibit ego. Such are the actions of the person who has risen to become detached from the three modes of Nature. One who gives up his false ego becomes free from the enigma of *samsara*. Instead of being attached to other persons and material possessions, the devotee develops his affection for the Supreme Lord, and sees Him everywhere.

The *Sharira Upanishad* states that the mind is positioned in the throat; intelligence in the face; ego in the heart; and *chitta,* or feelings, in the naval. In the waking state of existence, all organs are active. In the dreaming state, only the four subtle organs are active: (1) mind, (2) intelligence, (3) false ego, and (4) feeling. In deep sleep, only feeling remains. In the transcendental state of *turiya*, which is above all the mundane states of existence: waking, sleeping, and deep sleep, only the soul remains. According to the *Turyati Upanishad*, one who reaches the *avadhuta* state by becoming completely detached, attains the real position of the soul. The devotee who detaches himself from any actions that lead only to material goals, becomes qualified to vibrate the Holy Names of the Supreme Lord at all times.

One who is on the *avadutta* platform becomes desperate to realize the Absolute Truth, and remains always active. He is known as not only detached, but fearless, stable, highly intelligent, equal to all, modest, courageous, friendly, content, polite, inactive in action, and humble in speech. Because he always vibrates the Holy Names of

God, the devotee never submits to antagonism, since anger is born in the most subtle element of ether or *akasha*, whose attribute is sound. The attribute of *akasha* is emptiness, or "that which penetrates all other elements." However, for the devotee who always vibrates the Holy Names of the Lord, anger cannot arise out of lack or emptiness.

The process of chanting is described in the *Adhyatma Upanishad*: "The origin of sound through wind is called the penance of the heart." This original sound gains direct access to the mind, and uplifts the body by penetrating it. He who obtains mental power within his body becomes elevated to the supreme position. He who successfully attains the position of controlling his mind by meditating on the Supreme Lord in Krishna consciousness becomes liberated from the cycle of birth and death. Just as no outsider can blow out a lamp that has been lit inside another's house, so the defects of this world can never touch the witness within, who is unbiased and without any defect.

These Upanishadic truths reveal to the devotee that the original sound of the Hare Krishna *mahamantra* easily penetrates the mind, and thus uplifts the body. The Holy Names of the Lord release the mind from unnecessary distractions, such as the temptation to judge others. Then, when the devotee frees himself from mental defects, he obtains the liberated state of existence. His stable mind is never influenced by that which is external. At this point of enlightenment, the image of the spiritual reality becomes clear, and one can see himself immersed in Krishna consciousness, while the "ripples" that the mind causes soon disappear.

The devotee, through his mental stability, sees that both male and female energies exist within everything. For example, sometimes when there is a cloud, which is an expression of the male Savita, his feminine counterpart, or lightning, appears as Savitri. As explained in the *Savitri Upanishad,* whoever understands the essence of this truth may become liberated.

The *Pashupata Brahma Upanishad* states that purification of the mind must initially begin with a purified diet. Because Brahman is in everything, when one eats, he is without a doubt eating Brahman. The nature of Brahman is such that one makes whatever one wishes. Thus, if one eats the flesh of slaughtered animals, he likewise becomes dead. If one eats food offered to Brahman, meaning to the Source of Brahman or Lord Shri Krishna, then he becomes filled with the transcendental spiritual qualities of Brahman.

The *Atma Upanishad* describes the three types of souls:

(1) The gross soul that is embodied, and which revolves in the birth-and-death cycle of *samsara*;

(2) The inner soul that engages in the arts, knowledge, opinions and gender—and experiences the senses, forms attachment, and listens, and;

(3) The transcendental soul.

By understanding the transcendental soul, one attains liberation. One has to understand that this world is illusory, while the transcendental soul is eternal. The pure transcendental soul has no place of its own because it is part and parcel of the Supreme Lord Shri Krishna, who is situated everywhere. The Personality of Godhead is everywhere—He is beyond the duality of mundane knowledge and ignorance, and He is self-evident. This realization is an internal process. One who understands the nature of his soul, despite being engaged in ordinary activities, remains always detached. Although a mundane individual living in this material world might consider that the liberated person is no different from themselves, in fact, the *jivanmukta* is liberated even in this very lifetim

VI

The Avadhuta

To become a seeker of the Absolute, one should become an *avadhuta*. This means *a* (or immortal); *va* for *varenya* (or best); *dhu* (for freedom from worldly ties); and *ta* (or one who has attained *tattvamasi*, "I am that," or the understanding that he is part and parcel of the Supreme Lord. The *avadhuta* rises beyond the *varnas* and *ashramas,* or the four designations of social and spiritual orders. He moves perpetually and without attachment. Only one who is unaffected by the world can truly engage in magnanimous activities. These details are given in the *Avadhuta Upanishad*.

Additionally, the *Parabrahma Upanishad* states that, "One should resort to the internal thread of knowledge, instead of the external thread, or *yagnopavita,* that is worn by the *brahmana* class. One should resort to the internal *shikha* of OM, rather than to the external *shikha* tuft of hair." If the external attributes of a practitioner's appearance do not harmonize with internal realizations, then the dress becomes a mere show. To become liberated from birth and death, the sincere practitioner should preserve his energy by abstaining from the eight forms of sexual activity. As stated in *Katharudra Upanishad,* these eight are: (1) looking upon the objects of desire, (2) touching them, (3) playing with them, (4) discussing topics related to the object of desire, (5) conversing with the object of desire, (6) making a resolution to engage in sexual activities, (7) attempting to engage in sexual activity, and (8) the act of intercourse itself.

In *Rudrahridaya Upanishad,* Shrila Vyasadeva explains to his son Shukadeva Goswami, the essence of meditation by the liberated person. He states that Lord Vishnu is found in the harmony between Shiva and his consort Uma, and that a seer of the truth may see this harmony in everything. Vyasa gives his son the following examples: "The Sun is Shiva, while the shadow is Uma; the day is Shiva while the night is Uma; and the fragrance is Shiva while the flower is Uma. This harmony between them is an expression of Lord Vishnu. Whoever worships Lord Vishnu may attain the Supreme destination. The ordinary state of the soul in the material world is represented by Brahma; the higher soul of subtle experiences is represented by Shiva; and the everlasting state of the soul, the Supersoul, is represented by Bhagavan Vishnu." Thus, by understanding that "I am part and parcel of the Lord," the devotee extricates himself from the agony of material existence.

"The Sun is Shiva, while the shadow is Uma"

Discriminating between the individual soul, and the Soul of all souls, is based on illusion, or *maya*. In the spiritual world, this discrimination is under the decree of the goddess Yogamaya. There, she keeps the balance, and creates the harmony of love between both sides of the Absolute Truth, who are personified as Shri Radha and Krishna. While the mundane forms of the man and the woman are temporary because they are under the dictum of Mahamaya, everlasting love remains the only tangible reality that can be known by the liberated soul surrendered before the lotus feet of the Supreme Lord.

In the *Yoga-kundalini Upanishad,* it is described that, when one meditates on the loving relationship between the Lord and His energy, one may become a *jivanmukta,* or liberated soul, in this very life. When such a fortunate devotee gives up his mortal body, he becomes a *videha-mukta,* and obtains eternal liberation. In that state, only *rasa,* or the eternal loving relationship, remains present. In essence, the devotee's *rasas* with the Supreme Lord are five: (1) neutral, (2) servitude, (3) friendship, (4) parenthood, and (5) conjugal love. Although these five relationships are reflected within this material existence, here they lack agreement and are never eternal. On the other hand, in the spiritual world, such relationships stay eternal because of the harmony that exists there.

In this world, the embodied living entity is constantly troubled by diseases that result from sleeping during the day, late-night vigils, excessive sexual intercourse, moving in crowds, preventing the discharge of urine and feces, unwholesome food, and overexertion of *prana* (life force) due to mental strain. Additionally, the beginner on the path of *yoga* may also fall ill due to the cleansing away of his *anarthas,* or reactions to past sins, especially during the beginning of the process. Such a result can be discouraging to the neophyte *yogi,* and can cause him to relinquish his practice. Other discouraging factors can include doubts about the process, carelessness, laziness, excessive sleep, material attachments, erroneous perceptions (or illusion), pondering upon objects of the senses, lack of faith, and the inability to comprehend the Absolute Truth.

Each of the *Upanishads* provides the seeker with a somewhat different approach for attaining the Absolute Truth. Although it appears incredible that there are so many paths to self-realization, ultimately, they are one and the same because the goal is identical. Each of them facilitates a slightly different starting point for the practitioner, who is initially engrossed in different sorts of illusions. To the beginner, every *Upanishad* may appear like a different religious approach. However, they are all meant to lead the *yogi* to the highest level, which is accessible only to the most fortunate.

In the *Gopala Purvatapinya Upanishad,* Lord Brahma explains that the highest form of worship is devotion to Gopala Krishna. To that goal, he gives the Gopala and Kama Gayatri *mantras*, which are imparted unto the initiate at the time of *brahmana* initiation. Brahma explains that *krish* means "entity," and *na* means "pleasure." Thus, Krishna is the Embodiment of pleasure. Constant meditation upon the beautiful form of Lord Gopala Krishna in His abode of Goloka, where he sports with His cowherd boyfriends and girlfriends, the *gopas* and *gopis*, awards the devotee with ultimate liberation. Meditation upon Lord Shri Krishna is not difficult, since He is all-attractive by His beauty and activities. The best way to keep Shri Krishna in one's mind is through always chanting the Hare Krishna *mahamantra*.

The living entity has fallen into the pangs of material existence due to his forgetfulness of Shri Krishna. Here, in the world of *samsara*, we have diverted our focus away from the Supreme Lord Shri Krishna. Yet, the best way to return to our original position of eternity, knowledge, and bliss is through remembrance of Shri Krishna through keeping our focus on Him. Since repetition is the mother of remembrance, by chanting the Hare Krishna *mahamantra*, the devotee always remembers Shri Krishna, and never forgets Him. In this present age of Kali, the recommended process of self-realization is to chant:

Hare Krishna Hare Krishna Krishna Krishna Hare Hare,
Hare Rama Hare Rama Rama Rama Hare Hare

By this simple and attractive method, the devotee can regain his eternal constitutional position in Krishna's abode of bliss, where he becomes eternally engaged in the service of the Lord. In the *Krishna Upanishad,* it is stated that all demons, or obstacles on the path of self-realization, are destroyed simply by chanting the Holy Name of Shri Krishna.

Because Lord Shri Krishna and His devotees are inseparable, they appear to be part of Him. In the *Varaha Upanishad*, Shri Varaha, an incarnation of Lord Shri Krishna, states that He is the seat of love. He further explains how the concept of "mine" is the cause of bondage, while the concept of "I" is the cause of liberation. The concept of "mine and yours" creates feelings of envy that are responsible for our becoming separated from the Absolute. Thus, covetousness creates the karmic bondage that anchors the materialist to his illusions.

In the eternal world of Krishna, there is no waking state of existence, as one who is awake in the material sense always desires to make changes in himself and in the world around him. The spiritual world is completely free from hankering after the constant changes that are so prevalent in the waking state of existence in the material world. In the eternal world, there is no dreaming state since there is no sense of moving away, as one who is asleep in the material sense always wants to change his location. On the contrary, the spiritual reality is always in itself, and never changes its location, since it is perfect.

In the spiritual world, there is no dreamless state in which merging with Brahman occurs and, as a result, there is no awareness of the

Supreme Brahman. However, only by dint of his awareness of the existence of the Supreme Lord, does the *jiva* understand himself, and thus expresses his individuality. As a result, in the spiritual reality, the devotee is always aware that he is a person. Having gone there, he never desires to become somebody else, like Mayavadis here wish to become the Supreme Lord by merging into His existence. In deep sleep, one merges within the existence of the Supreme, and by losing his own personality, experiences the impersonal aspect of the Absolute. However, when one has dived deeply into the transcendental state of existence of the self, one associates with the Supreme Self or the all-attractive Lord Shri Krishna. This state is beyond mundane pain and pleasure, and is beyond the waking, dreaming, and deep sleep states of existence in the material world.

This transcendental state is easily achieved through constantly chanting the Hare Krishna *mahamantra* since, through this process, one directly engages the mind in the contemplation of Bhagavan. This process is beyond speech as speech is subject to a beginning and end. In the eye of the *atmajnani,* "the knower of the self," mystic powers or *siddhis* are insignificant. *Siddhis* are obtained through medicine, wealth, chanting of *mantras*, religious work, investment of time, and skill. The *atmajnani* is a *jivanmukta,* because he has become liberated even within this body.

Although there are different levels of *jivanmukta*, all of them lead to the final state. Therefore, even in the preliminary stage, one may be considered liberated. The first stage of *jivanmukta* starts with the intent to become liberated. Next, one seeks the truth from a proper source. Then, through practice, the seeker settles into *sattva guna,* or goodness. After that, he develops non-attachment to the world. Attaining the next stage, he learns to properly analyze every object. The final stage is pure transcendental realization.

At first, the practitioner identifies with the gross waking state. Then, he identifies with the subtle reality, which is represented by dreaming. Next, one identifies with the dreamless state of existence when one merges into Brahman. The self-aware one realizes in that state that his intelligence is part and parcel of the intelligence of the Supreme Lord, and since everything belongs to Shri Krishna, he recognizes that he is not the owner even of his own soul. Having understood the mundane existence and its various stages, he goes beyond to realize his own personality in relationship to the Lord. That is called the *turiya* state, which is complete, and beyond the limitations of mundane explanations.

The *Kali Santarana Upanishad* informs us that, at the end of Dwapara Yuga, Narada Muni approached his father Lord Brahma, the first living entity of the universe. Lord Brahma is also the head of all the Vaishnavas in our Brahma-Madhava-Gaudiya *sampradaya*.

Narada inquired from Lord Brahma about the means of crossing over the ocean of Kali Yuga, which lasts for 432,000 years. Lord Brahma simply replied that there is only one way to overcome the pangs of this age, and that is through the chanting of the names of Lord Narayana. Then, in the following arrangement of syllables, Lord Brahma chanted the *mahamantra* as the world's only means of deliverance:

Hare Rama Hare Rama Rama Rama Hare Hare
Hare Krishna Hare Krishna Krishna Krishna Hare Hare.

Later in Kali Yuga, Krishna in His full incarnation as Shri Chaitanya Mahaprabhu, reversed the order of the *mahamantra*. Even so, there are still some practitioners who begin chanting the *mantra* with "Hare Rama."

Narada Muni then asked his father about the proper means of conducting the chanting, to which Lord Brahma surprised him by replying that there are none. One can chant while he is in a pure state, or even in an impure state. Because there are no hard and fast rules for chanting, by continuing the process, all good results will manifest. Then, the imaginary or body-conscious personality that the *atma* deluded by maya has created, will disappear, and Parabrahman, the original state of existence, will emanate from within. Lord Brahma explained to Narada that the practitioner can become liberated after repeating the *mantra* thirty-five million times. That comes to approximately sixty years of daily chanting the recommended sixteen rounds of the *mahamantra* on a *mala* of 108 beads. Shrila Prabhupada recommended chanting a minimum of sixteen rounds daily, but since there are no hard and fast rules for chanting, the devotee who chants additional rounds lowers the time margin advised by Lord Brahma.

Meditation upon the holy names of the Lord can be either *savikalpa* or *nirvikalpa*. In the beginning, the practitioner mediates on the *mantra* by associating it with the form of the Deity, and by hearing His pastimes. That is called the *savikalpa* process. However, when the chanter progresses, he begins to hear the names of the Lord deeply within himself, emanating directly from his heart. At this *nirvikalpa* stage, he is no longer distracted by the external forms of matter. Rather, he plunges into the reality of the eternal self within. *Nirvikalpa* meditation leads to *samadhi,* or complete transcendence of the mundane reality. The advanced devotee does not experience any disorientation while simultaneously observing the mundane and the transcendental states of existence.

The necessity to know both the mundane and the transcendental at the same time as they are both art and parcel of Shri Krishna is further explained in *Shri Ishopanishad* (11), "Only one who can learn the process of nescience, and that of transcendental knowledge, side by side can transcend the influence of repeated birth and death, and enjoy the full blessings of immortality."

According to the *Sarasvati-Rahasya Upanishad*, there are four types of sound. (1) *Para* is the primeval sound, which is actually the name of God. (2) *Pashyanti* is the sound that is heard in deep mediation. (3) *Madhyama* is the sound translated into an idea. Finally, (4) *vaikhari* is the spoken sound in the form of speech. One who merely utters the names of God without any viable realization is merely manufacturing sounds of meaningless repetition, like a parrot. In the *madhyama,* or medium stage of sound, one can start understanding the metaphysical properties of the *mahamantra*, although he is still on the philosophical level of understanding. The sound of the Hare Krishna *mahamantra* automatically vibrates in the heart of the partitioner who becomes advanced in the *pashyanti* realization of sound. Such a devotee encounters no problem meditating on the holy names of the Lord, because of the constant flow of transcendental vibrations from his heart. In the *para* stage of sound, no other sounds remain in the heart, except the names of God.

Lord Ramachandra instructs Hanuman

In the *Muktika Upanishad*, Lord Ramachandra instructs Hanuman about the process of liberation. *Salokya mukti*, or living on the same planet as the Lord, is obtained through chanting of His holy names, and by living in a holy place. *Sarupya mukti,* or having the same body as the Lord, is obtained through living in a holy place, chanting His names, and meditating upon His Deity form. *Sarshti mukti,* or having the same opulence as the Lord, is obtained through serving Him. Lastly, *samipya mukti,* or personal association, is attained through undivided attention upon the Lord. Lord Ramachandra has not mentioned *sayujya mukti,* since merging into the existence of the Lord is impersonal liberation, and is compared to spiritual suicide.

The materialistic consciousness of the conditioned soul is prone to enjoyment that only creates pain and bondage. By controlling the attitude of enjoyment, the aspirant can rise to become a *jivanmukta,* or liberated soul. *Videha mukti,* or final liberation after death, occurs through the extinguishing *prarabdha,* or the collective results of past *karma.* This cleansing process of the soul results in removing all vehicles—or bodies—that are held by the individual *jiva.*

Furthermore, Lord Rama explains to Hanuman the means of obtaining eternal bliss. Just as progeny can be obtained through performing the *putrakameshti yagna*; or as wealth can be obtained through trade; or as heaven can be obtained through the *jyotishtoma yagna*; so the *jivanmukta* state can be obtained through *samadhi* received through the study of *Vedanta* or the conclusions of the *Vedas.*

The general efforts of men are of two types: (1) those that in accordance with scripture and lead to self-realization, and (2) those that are not in accordance with scripture and lead to bondage. The mind that associates with the *vasanas*—or the karmic imprint upon the mind that results in impressions and desires—tends to bondage. On the other hand, the mind that is disassociated from such karmic imprints becomes liberated. *Vasanas* arise through the false identification of the self with sense objects. This happens when one meditates on the objects of the senses, whether in friendly or adverse ways. The *jiva* soul's bondage to material existence arises not only through *vasana,* but through the vibrations that are created through breathing. Should one of them perish, the other will soon perish as well.

If the seeker is unable to practice the cessation of his breathing through the *yoga* process, then he can destroy the *vasanas* through becoming detached from work, through abandoning the concept that this perishable world is the reality, and through understanding that he is not the physical body. One whose mind forgoes attachment to the *vasanas* finds everlasting peace without anxiety, the state of ultimate reality.

This cessation of *vasanas* can be achieved either (1) through associating with seers who have already achieved this state, or (2) by controlling one's *prana* under the direction of an adept, who has achieved the ultimate state. Since *vasanas* imply longing for objects of sense pleasure, such impure desires lead to bondage; while attachment to the Supreme Lord Narayana leads to salvation.

The *atma* is originally pure, while the body is impure. When the seeker understands the difference between the two, then he becomes purified. The materialistic person who thinks that the body is the self becomes a victim of time, and is no longer a *jivanmukta* or liberated soul. The *Amritabindu Upanishad* states that the body itself is blind to its own inevitable destruction, because only the eternal *atma* can be a witness to the body's end. Although self-realization can be obtained through the *Vedas*, the adept abandons even the *Vedas* once his goal is achieved. Self-realization is indeed latent in every being, and the liberated person sees and associates only with that potential in everyone. Thus, in the *Svayamvedyo Upanishad,* it is stated that the liberated person sees everyone with equal vision. His loyalty is only to the one Paramatma Who is within everyone and everything.

VII

Salvation from Delusion

All living entities in the material world are in delusion, The demigods, for example, long to be worshipped, although they can be cheated even by their worshipers. Other living entities who present themselves as teachers are also in delusion. The scholars of *shastra* who lack genuine realization are also confused. Other living entities embark on pilgrimage and hope for the essence there. Some living entities perform great deeds thinking that is the essence of life. Still, other individuals think of themselves as having become God. Some think of themselves as being blessed by a deity with the power to recover lost objects, or to visualize the destinies of others. There are others who present themselves as worshipers of the all-pervasive Lord Vishnu, although, being proud of their positions, they remain morose and thus go to hell—even after declaring themselves to be the best of devotees. The average individual within the masses is mired deeply in ignorance, while still others—including the scientists and the metaphysicians—like to argue with one another based on their own imaginary opinions of the world. Still other living entities, those in the bodies of animals, do not care for all of the above, but are found at the same places where the demigods and humans reside, and are also confused by ignorance. Those that are not confused are rare, as Shri Krishna states in *Bhagavad-gita As It Is* (7.9):

bahunam janmanam ante
jnanavān mam prapadyate
vasudevaḥ sarvam iti
sa mahatma su-durlabhah

"After many births and deaths, he who is actually in knowledge surrenders unto Me, knowing Me to be the cause of all causes and all that is. Such a great soul is very rare."

All groups of living entities long for their true nature, which can only be found when one abandons all duality and achieves equal vision. The exception to this concept is the disciple's reverence for Shri Guru, because the spiritual master is viewed as the highest and above all. The spiritual master must always be revered with a special vision. One should abandon duality and have an equal vision for everybody but the *guru*. This vision is the true meaning of duality. The fortunate soul gets Shri Guru by the mercy of Shri Krishna, and by the mercy of Shri Guru one gets Krishna. Since the bona fide spiritual master is none other than a true representative of Shri Krishna, it is only through his mercy that the disciple can understand the self, and the eternal function of the soul as Krishna's servant.

In *Chaitanya Charitamrita* (Madhya19.151) it is stated:

> *brahmaṇḍa bhramite kona bhagyavan jiva*
> *guru-krishna-prasade paya bhakti-lata-bija*

"According to their *karma*, all living entities are wandering throughout the entire universe. Some of them are being elevated to the upper planetary systems, and some are going down into the lower planetary systems. Out of many millions of wandering living entities, one who is very fortunate gets an opportunity to associate with a bona fide spiritual master by the grace of Krishna. By the mercy of both Krishna and the spiritual master, such a person receives the seed of the creeper of devotional service."

In the *Mantrika Upanishad,* the soul is described as invisible, although it can be "seen" through its devotion, knowledge, and action. The eternal pure spirit soul is beyond the three *gunas* of goodness (*satya-guna*), passion (*raja-guna*), and ignorance (*tamo-*

guna). Those entities who are in illusion milk the allegorical cow of nature, and they receive as their reward different "milk" in the form of either goodness, passion, or ignorance.

The Supreme Lord, through His meditation and detachment, enjoys the illusory world, which is His reflection. In this way, the Lord prolongs the existence of this world. Those who are in knowledge observe the Personality of Godhead Vishnu even in the "illusive realities" of this universe. This Supreme Person is celibate and undivided like a pillar. He is full of worldly fruit and opulence. He is the support of the *yantra* ("machine") of this world. Although He is void of *rajas* or passion, He is enriched by *sattva,* or goodness. He is seen through His universal form. He is time itself, and the breath of all entities. Although He is seen in the great demigods who control the natural elements, His powers are also seen in the great demons. The Lord is Nirguna, or "beyond any material definition." He is in everything, and He is the knower of all causes and effects.

A devotee of the Lord may also obtain an invisible form, just as the Lord Himself, and enjoy transcendental pleasure. Some view the Lord as undivided; while others see Him as Shiva and Shakti, or the combined male and female aspect of everything. Still others see Him as Brahma, Vishnu, and Maheshwara, the Trimurti, who embodies creation, maintenance, and destruction of the material universe. Others think of Him as the combination of Brahma, Vishnu and Maheshvara along with Gauri and Ganesh who is always expanding His transcendental pastimes.

One can meditate on the Lord of this world, yet, there is another world of Vaikuntha, whose nucleus is Goloka Vrindavana. There, the devotee is not distracted by the trivialities of the temporary world, and he engages in eternal service to Shri Shri

Radha-Krishna. As stated in the *Tusalya Upanishad*, this service is further facilitated in this world by Tulasi devi, the beloved plant of Lord Vishnu, Chanting the Hare Krishna *mahamantra* on Tulsi beads destroys all poverty, while honoring its leaves as *prasad* empowers breathing. Evil is destroyed by spreading on oneself the clay from the place where she grows. One should not pluck her leaves whimsically, but always with proper intention. She should not be touched at night, and not plucked on days of festivals and celebrations. By doing so, one creates animosity with Lord Vishnu. If a *brahmana* does not know this, he is compared to a *chandala,* or an evildoer.

Tulasi devi is dear to the Lord, and she is a friend to His consort Lakshmidevi. The whole auspiciousness resides in Tulasi devi, and wherever she grows is considered Vrindavana, the residence of Lord Shri Krishna. One should circle Tulasi devi whenever he sees her. No *sraddha* ceremony (oblations to the departed), or worship of any demigod, is sufficient without a Tulasi leaf. If such ceremonies lack Tulasi leaves, they are considered to be offerings to a demon. A garland of Tulasi leaves and flowers gives all wealth and auspiciousness. By worshiping her, one attains Vaikuntha.

The *Tusalya Upanishad* further mentions that chanting the Upanishadic *shlokas* gives the result of worshiping Tulasi devi because of their specific rhyme and meter. Thus, the different Upanishadic rhymes control breathing in certain ways, and one who recites them gains particular results. The chanting of the Hare Krishna *mahamantra* is also encoded in such a rhyme and rhythm so that the person who chants it can gain all the desired effects very quickly, and soon his original position will be revealed.

VIII

The Gayatri Mantra

In the *Chaturaveda Upanishad*, it is explained that the four *Vedas* became manifested by Lord Narayana through Lord Brahma, at the time when he mediated in the four different directions of the world. Lord Brahma has four heads, and each of the four *Vedas* originate from different face of Brahma. In the auspisioust eastern direction, the first *Rig Veda* and Gayatri *mantra* were generated. The *Vedas* are not mere books because they were first spoken, and were written down much later. They are the very acts of manifestation of the world with its different steps. The *Vedas* first manifested with the manifestation of the world. Only later, were they written down to be immortalized and remembered. Thus, whoever uses them in an unadulterated way also can manifest just like Lord Brahma, who created the universe with pure intentions.

The Gayatri *mantra* is the original hymn, and it consists of twenty-four syllables in which the entire creation is described and rests. Gayatri is the hymn of the inner essence of the Sun or, Surya-Narayana, who is the primeval light of the spiritual reality revealed in this manifested world. By realizing the meaning of the Gayatri *mantra*, one can see that Lord Narayana is in everything, and that He is the active principle, the inner sun of the soul and the pillar of this world. In Gayatri, not only are positive attributes encoded, but also the twenty-four sins. By chanting the Gayatri *mantra*, one can overcome every sin, whether created knowingly or unknowingly.

However, one should know that he can effectively receive the Gayatri *mantra* only from a qualified *brahmana,* who has realized the potency of Gayatri in full.

The twenty-four sins mentioned in the *Gayatri-rahasya Upanishad* are:

1. Cow slaughter,

2. Murder of a *brahmana*,

3. Abortion, or murder of the unborn living entity,

4. Murder of a brother,

5. Murder of a person,

6. Murders committed in many previous births, and mass murder,

7. Murder of the wife,

8. Murder of the teacher,

9. Murder of the father,

10. Suicide, or murder of one's self,

11. Murder of living organisms, whether movable or immovable,

12. Eating of living organisms that are moving or unmoving, after killing them,

13. Murder arising after eating prohibited and unclean substances,

14. Evils resulting from accepting and misusing donations,

15. Abandoning one's duty.

16. Evils arising due to not complying with the duties assigned by one's employer, which includes misdeeds performed in the name of

God, who is the true owner or employer of everyone,

17. Theft of another's wealth,

18. Evils arising due to eating food cooked by an obnoxious person (the emotions of the cook are embedded in the food, and affect the person who eats it),

19. Negative results due to attacking an enemy,

20. Enjoyment of sexual union with a low-class person, who is unclean internally or externally,

21. Any evil acts that are performed due to ignorance,

22. Guilty pleasures (evils done due to inability to control the mind),

23. Heinous evils (evil activities that have been pre-planned),

24. Illicit sexual union.

The initiation into becoming a *brahmana* makes one twice-born, or reborn into the spiritual reality.

IX

The Four Varnas and Ashramas

As mentioned in *Bhagavad-gita As It Is* (4.13), the society of four *varnas* and four *ashramas* were created by Shri Krishna Himself:

*chatur-varnyam maya sristam guna-karma vibhagashah
tasya kartaram api mam viddhy akartaram avyayam*

"According to the three modes of material nature, and the work ascribed to them, the four divisions of human society were created by Me. And, although I am the creator of this system, you should know that I am yet the non-doer, being unchangeable."

Krishna has created these four *ashramas* to give ultimate success in spiritual realization, and to progress sinlessly in accordance with the laws of *dharma*. In the *Ashrama Upanishad,* there is a very good elaboration of the four basic *ashrams*, or spiritual levels of life: (1)

brahmachari ashram for the celibate student residing in the *ashram* of the *guru*; (2) *grihasta ashram,* or marriage; (3) *vanaprastha ashram,* or withdrawing from active marriage; and (4) *sannyasa ashram,* or full renunciation.

The first level, or *brahmacharya,* has four levels. The first level is the *gayatra*, when the student who, after receiving his *brahmana* thread, chants the Gayatri *mantra* for four days and nights and without taking any salt in his food.

At the second level, the student engages himself for twelve years in the studies of the *Veda,s* while observing celibacy. Thus, he is called a *brahmana*.

At the third level, he marries, although he has sexual relations with his wife only after her period, and for purposes of procreation. Such a man is called a *prajapatya*. A householder who successfully practices sense restraint is also considered a *brahmachari*.

At the fourth level, the perfect student, who does not leave his teacher throughout his life, is known as a *brihan*.

The householder, or self-controlled *grihasta*, is also of four types:

The first type of householder, or *vartaka-vritti*, engages in agriculture, animal husbandry, and business activities that are performed according to the laws of his land. Such a *vartaka-vritti* may worship the Lord's Deity in a temple meant for public worship.

Next, the second type, or moderate householder is called *salina-vritti*. He purposely distances himself from society, and makes his offerings to the Lord in private. Although such a *salina-vritti* householder engages in study the *Vedas*, he does not teach. He may provide gifts, although he does not accept any.

The third type of *grihasta* is the *yayavara,* who has no fixed abode. The *yayavara* prepares offerings for the Lord, and engages others in the same activity. The *yayavara* shares his education with others. Since it is the nature of the *yayavara* to perform sacrifices, he may accept as well as give gifts.

Lastly, the *ghora-samnyasin grihastas* drink only water, while surviving only on grains that have fallen onto the ground, and without storing them. They worship the Lord through their acts of renunciation.

Married men that do not follow any such restrictions in household life, and who live just to satisfy their own senses, are called *grihamedis*. Such *grihamedis,* that cohabit with their wives solely for their own sense gratification, are the prominent type of householder in the world today. Even so, such *grihamedis* are superior to miscreants who are addicted to illicit sex without the tie of marriage, and who only produce unwanted population.

Among *vanaprasthis,* the *vaikhanasa* lives in the forest and survives on grains that he grows himself. The *vaikhanasa* takes medicines and vegetables that have been left aside by other people. The *vanaprasti vaikhanasa* daily worships the *devatas* (demigods), the *pitris* (ancestors), the *bhutas* (subtle spirits), the *manushyas* (humans), and the *brahmanas* who are versed in Vedic knowledge.

The *udumbara vanaprastis* are those who wake up early in the morning and perform the worship of the five above-mentioned living entities with offerings of figs from the rare *udumbara* tree, and other rare flowers and fruits.

The *vanaprasti* who dresses in the skin of an animal or in the bark of a tree; who keeps matted hair; and who eats fruits and flowers without accumulating them during the four holy months of *chaturamasya,* is called the *balakhilya*. Once Kartika-*masa,* the final month of *chaturamasya* is over, the *balakhilya* returns to earning his living even as he continues to perform the above-mentioned ceremonies.

The *vanaprasthi* who lives wherever he can find a place, eats thorns and leaves, and does the above-mentioned ceremonies is called the *phenap*.

Sannyasa, or the renounced order, is also divided into four stages:

The first stage is the *kutichaka.* Although a *kutichaka sannyasi* has renounced the world, he may survive on alms offered by his children.

The second type, or *bahudaka sannyasi,* survives by begging alms from the houses of respected *brahmanas*. The *bahudaka sannyasi* wears a *brahmana* thread, has a *shikha* (tuft of hair on the head), carries a bag and a sitting mat, uses footwear, has a vessel for water, and holds a *danda*.

The third type of *sannyasa* is the *hamsa*. He is a recluse who keeps long hair, wears a *brahmana* thread, carries a bag and a water pot and holds a *danda*. The *hamsa* stays in a village for a single night, and in a city for five nights, and performs penance by fasting.

The fourth and final stage of *sannyasa* is the *paramahamsa,* who has renounced all possessions. He shaves his head completely, and wears only two garments: a cloth to tie up his private parts, and another cloth for the upper body. Although he never uses intoxicants, he may appear intoxicated. He may either live in an abandoned house, or silently wander here and there, living on alms. He sees everyone with equal vision, and endeavors to free his soul from *samsara*. The *paramahamsa* understands that nothing belongs to him, because he is fully focused on the relationship between the self and the Supreme Self.

The *sannyasi* who abandons the vows of the order of renunciation is compared to the killer of a *brahmana*, to the killer of an embryo, to the destroyer of a spiritually-oriented enterprise, or to other heinous criminals. The student who foregoes his loyalty to Lord Vishnu is considered to have become a thief. A regular sinner can overcome his sins through lamenting his misdeeds. However, one who abandons renunciation may never regain his position.

X

The Deepest Secret of All

A student who does not properly honor his spiritual master, and who shows such a disrespectful attitude in his mind, his speech, and his actions, receives only a worthless and illusory education. The spiritual teacher embodies the personification of the supreme religion, and the supreme position of existence. Any knowledge that has been acquired by the student who is offensive toward his teacher becomes gradually diminished. However, the disciple who offers his obeisance equally to his teacher, and to the Supreme Lord, becomes the best of devotees. As told in the *Satyayaniya Upanishad*, simply due to his proper attitude, such a worthy disciple attains his supreme destination.

The deepest secret of all is revealed by Lord Bramha in the *Radha Upanishad*. Shri Krishna is the Lord of lords. He has unlimited potencies including *hladini*, *sandhini*, *jnana*, *iccha*, and *kriya*. The prime potency is Hladini who is personified as Radhika, because Shri Krishna worships Her. She is the Supreme Goddess Who controls the very breath of Lord Shri Krishna. Therefore, it is stated there that only fools worship Shri Krishna without Shri Radha.

Studying the *Upanishads* should never be undertaken without the guidance of a bona fide Vaishnava *guru*. Without the direction of a proper devotee guide, the result of whimsical interpretation will be only mental speculation, and it will give the opposite of the intended effect. Therefore, our spiritual master, His Divine Grace A.C. Bhaktivedanta Swami Prabhupada, has recommended that the sincere student should first undertake a step-by-step study of the verses of his *Shri Ishopanishad*. The student who seeks the genuine process of self-realization may next study Shrila Prabhupada's *Bhagavad-gita As It Is*. Spoken on the Battlefield of Kurukshetra by the Supreme  Personality of Godhead Krishna to his disciple Arjuna, the *Gita*, or the *Gitopanishad*, condenses all Upanishadic wisdom into seven hundred verses. In the *Bhagavad-gita,* Lord Krishna explains the ultimate message of enlightenment, or pure devotional service in Krishna consciousness.

OM TAT SAT

16 June 2024

Abhaya Ashram, Blagoevgrad

Afterword

Originally, there were more than one thousand Upanishads, of which 108 are still known today. Still, the sheer quantity and volume can be bewildering. This book – Light of the Upanishads – has the potential of "de-wildering" the reader.

Quite obviously, I only speak from my own experience reading this illuminating book. This is an afterword after all and not a review so like to share a few things that particularly stand out for me personally.

The language of the author Abhaya Mudra Devi Dasi is refreshingly lucid. Everything becomes very clear. At no point is the reader left guessing. This is very much in line with the supremely clear language of His Divine Grace A.C. Bhaktivedanta Swami Prabhupada. Furthermore, the entire book is concise – which is quite an achievement – a summary and conclusion of all Upanishads in under 100 pages.

A most wonderful thing is that the book written for all levels of readers. A serious beginner will get all the guidance required in her or his quest for bhakti. The intermediate sincere student will be relieved of all remaining impersonal contamination, and the more advanced reader will get many misunderstandings dissolved, and see the essence of all revealed scriptures in a new light with horizons expanding. Please note that these are just a few points and by no means a complete assessment.

One amazing experience I had while reading this book was that I received profound answers not only to questions that I consciously had – but to questions that I was not even aware of as well.

Is Light of the Upanishads a scholarly work? Yes. But not for the sake of scholarship in itself. Being thoroughly unpretentious by nature, Abhaya Mudra Devi Dasi is very practical – a sincere reader can apply everything learned directly to her or his daily life and meditation. Moreover, since the author is a realized and genuine Vaishnava devotee the book carries all the potency of literature that are in line with guru, sadhu, and shastra.

I am especially happy that two essential points are emphasized through all chapters. The eradication of any trace of impersonal contamination – and the inestimable importance of chanting the Mahamantra above any other practice in this age.

I like to conclude with re-quoting Mantra 16 of the Shri Ishopanishad, which already appeared in the Introduction of this work:

"O my Lord, O primeval philosopher, maintainer of the universe, O regulating principle, destination of the pure devotees, well-wisher of the progenitors of mankind, please remove the effulgence of Your transcendental rays so that I can see Your form of bliss. You are the eternal Supreme Personality of Godhead, like unto the sun, as am I."

The Shri Ishopanishad was the very first genuine book of divine knowledge that I read, at hte age of 15. This Mantra 16 changed my entire life. What a relief it was and what a heavy load was taken off me – the Absolute Truth is personal after all!

May this much needed book reach as many souls as possible for their benefit and enlightenment. It has the potential to change the life of the sincere reader for good – by turning towards the Supreme Personality of Godhead Shri Krishna.

Avadhuta Das Goswami

Bibliography

Bhaktivedanta Swami, A.C. *Bhagavad-gita As It Is*, 1972, Bhakivedanta Book Trust

Bhaktivedanta Swami, A.C. *Chaitanya Charitamrita* 1975, Bhakivedanta Book Trust, Los Angeles.

Bhaktivedanta Swami, A.C. *Nectar of Devotion*, 1970, ISKCON Press, Boston

Bhaktivedanta Swami, A.C. *Shri Ishopanishad*, 1974, Bhakivedanta Book Trust, Los Angeles.

Bhaktivedanta Swami, A.C. *Shrimad-Bhagavatam*, 1976, Bhakivedanta Book Trust, Los Angeles.

Board of Scholars, K.L. Joshi et al., *112 Upanisads*, vols 1 & 2, 5th edition, 2016, Parimal Publications, Delhi

www.ingramcontent.com/pod-product-compliance
Lightning Source LLC
Chambersburg PA
CBHW041523090426
42737CB00037B/14